You Are There

Cities

The Building of America

Reading Consultant   Linda Cornell, Learning Resource Consultant, Indiana Department of Education

Acknowledgments:

Product Development	Gare Thompson Associates
Design	Carlos Gaudier
Production	Silver Editions
Editor	Monica Halpern
Research	Beverly Mitchell

Photo Credits:
Cover (top left), Images © 1996 PhotoDisc, Inc.; cover (top right), © Dave Mitchell/Photographer; cover (bottom left), Images © 1996 PhotoDisc, Inc.; cover (bottom center; bottom right), Library of Congress; 3 (left; inset), Library of Congress; 4 (left; right), Library of Congress; 4 (center), Images © 1996 PhotoDisc, Inc.; 5 (top left; bottom center), Library of Congress; 5 (top center), John F. Kennedy Library; 5 (right), © Ena Keo/Photographer; 6 (top right; bottom left; bottom right), Library of Congress; 7 (top center), Images © 1996 PhotoDisc, Inc.; 7 (bottom left; bottom center), Library of Congress; 7 (bottom right), Images © 1996 PhotoDisc, Inc.; 8 (top; bottom), Images © 1996 PhotoDisc, Inc.; 9 (left), © Frank Cezus/Tony Stone Images; 9 (inset), Library of Congress; 10 (left; right), Library of Congress; 11 (top), Library of Congress; 11 (bottom center) © Robert Kusel/Tony Stone Images; 11 (bottom right), © Frank Cezus/Tony Stone Images; 12 (left; center; right), Library of Congress; 13 (left; center), Library of Congress; 13 (right), © Nigel Snowdon/Tony Stone Images; 14 (left; right), Images © 1996 PhotoDisc, Inc.; 15 (left; inset), Images © 1996 PhotoDisc, Inc.; 16 (left), Library of Congress; 16 (center), UPI/Corbis-Bettmann; 16 (right), White House Historical Society; 17 (top), Images © 1996 PhotoDisc, Inc.; 17 (bottom), Library of Congress; 18 (left; right), Library of Congress; 18 (center), Images © 1996 PhotoDisc, Inc.; 19 (left) Images © 1996 PhotoDisc, Inc.; 19 (center), © David Frazier/Tony Stone Images; 19 (right), © Randy Wells/Tony Stone Images; 20 (top), © Jeff Greenberg/Peter Arnold, Inc.; 20 (bottom), Images © 1996 PhotoDisc, Inc.; 21 (left), Images © 1996 PhotoDisc, Inc.; 21 (inset), © Jeff Greenberg/Peter Arnold, Inc.; 22 (left; right), Library of Congress; 22 (center), Courtesy of the Dallas Convention & Visitors Bureau; 23 (top left), Library of Congress; 23 (top right; bottom left), Courtesy of the Dallas Convention & Visitors Bureau; 24 (top), Library of Congress; 24 (bottom), © Helene Slavens/Peter Arnold, Inc.; 25 (left), UPI/Corbiss-Bettman; 25 (center), © Jeff Greenberg/Peter Arnold, Inc.; 25 (right), © Ena Keo/Photographer; 26 (top), © Clay Kelton/Peter Arnold, Inc.; 26 (bottom), © Jeff Greenberg/Peter Arnold, Inc.; 27 (left), Images © 1996 PhotoDisc, Inc.; 27 (inset), © Vince Streano/Tony Stone Images; 28 (left; center), Library of Congress; 28 (right), Images © 1996 PhotoDisc, Inc.; 29 (left; right), Library of Congress; 30 (left), Library of Congress; 30 (right), © Vince Streano/Tony Stone Images; 31 (left), © Matthew McVay/Tony Stone Images; 31 (top right), Images © 1996 PhotoDisc, Inc.; 31 (bottom right), Images © 1996 PhotoDisc, Inc.; 32 (left), © Richard Choy/Peter Arnold, Inc.; 32 (right), © Dave Mitchell/Photographer.

Library of Congress Cataloging-in-Publication Data

Thompson, Gare.
Cities : the building of America / by Gare Thompson ; photographer, Martin W. Sandler.
p.   cm. -- (You are there)
Summary: Supplies interesting facts about the building and history of America's cities.
ISBN 0-516-20701-6 (lib. bdg.) ISBN 0-516-26058-8 (pbk.)
1. Cities and towns--United States--History-Case studies--Juvenile literature. [1. Cities and towns--History.]
I. Sandler, Martin W., ill. II. Title. III. Series: You are there (Danbury, Conn.)
HT123.T46 1997
307.76'0973--dc21   96-51976
                                                                     CIP
                                                                     AC

Boston and New York City

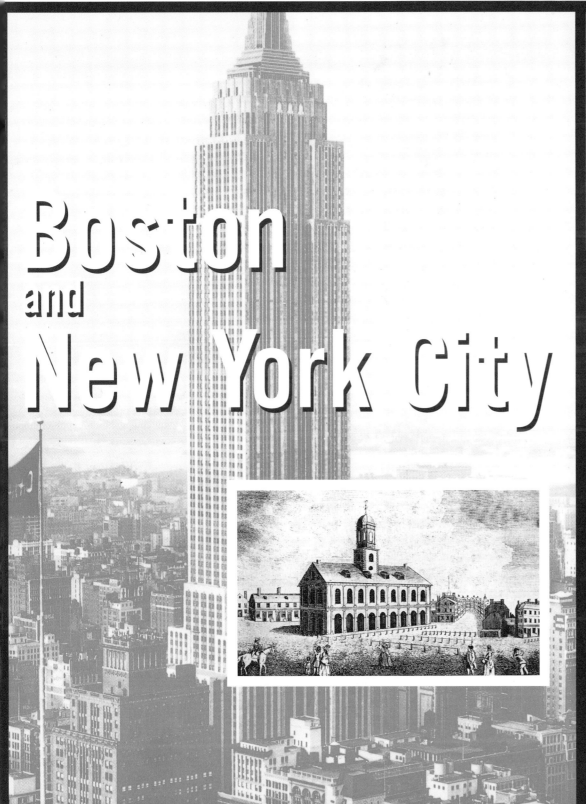

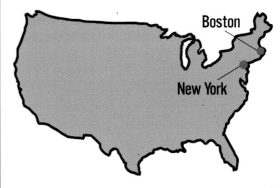

Boston and New York City were early American harbor cities. They were built around harbors that led into the Atlantic Ocean. Ships brought goods and people in and out of these cities easily. Both cities became important centers of colonial life.

Boston... a city rich in history

The Boston Tea Party

Great Britain ruled over the American colonies in its early years. The British made laws that the colonists hated. One law placed a tax on tea. Tea was a favorite drink of the colonists. In 1773, furious pro-testers dumped 342 chests of tea into Boston Harbor. This protest was called the Boston Tea Party.

One if by Land, Two if by Sea

The British troops decided to attack Boston. Paul Revere rode his horse to warn the people that the British were coming. He was also a famous silversmith.

Did you know?

Crispus Attucks, an African-American, fought and died in the Boston Massacre (March 5, 1770).

Protesters dump tea into Boston Harbor.

Statue of Paul Revere

Dr. Martin Luther King, Jr.

President Kennedy

Boston Today

Today Boston has a number of new buildings such as the John Hancock Building. It has many glass windows. An old church is reflected in its windows. Boston is a city rich in history, but it continues to change and grow.

The John Hancock Building

Learning and More Learning

There are many colleges in the Boston area. Harvard University is the oldest college in the United States. It was founded in 1636. Many famous people have gone to school in Boston. Dr. Martin Luther King, Jr. went to Boston University.

Politics, Sports, and Cooking

Many famous people are from or have lived in Boston. President John F. Kennedy was born there. John L. Sullivan, the boxer, and Ted Williams, the baseball player, were from Boston. Fannie Farmer, the author of a famous cookbook, also lived in Boston. Politics, sports, and cooking are still important in Boston.

Did you know?

The Boston Public Library is the oldest free public library in the United States. Students use this library to study.

5

New York... a city of many different people

From New Amsterdam to New York

The Dutch bought the island of Manhattan from the Indians for $24.00. They called the settlement they built there New Amsterdam.

In 1664, the British took over the Dutch city. They renamed it New York. George Washington was sworn in as our first president in New York City.

East Side, West Side, Uptown, Downtown

New York City became a city where all kinds of goods were sold. People filled the streets, buying and selling goods.

Every part of the city was special in its own way. Clothes were made on Seventh Avenue. The rich shopped on Fifth Avenue. The theaters were on Broadway. Stocks were bought and sold on Wall Street.

The streets in New York were always busy.

George Washington

People enjoying Central Park

Did you know?

Central Park is in the center of New York City. It covers 840 acres. Today people still enjoy skating, walking, and seeing plays and concerts in the park.

The twin towers of the World Trade Center are now the tallest buildings in New York City.

The World Trade Center

Give Me Your Tired, Your Poor...

One of the most famous landmarks of New York City is the Statue of Liberty. Given to the United States by the French people in 1886, it stands for freedom. The statue was often the first sight of America for the people who passed through New York Harbor and landed in New York City.

The City of Skyscrapers

Many tall buildings were built in New York City. One of its most famous buildings is the Empire State Building. When it was completed in 1931, it was 1,250 feet high. It remained the tallest building in the world until 1971. Today it still is a major tourist site.

The Empire State Building in New York

Arts and Artists

New York City has long been a center for the arts. Dance companies, art galleries, and theater companies show artists' work. Writers, dancers, singers, actors, and artists of every kind come to New York to try to "make it" or find success. There is a saying that you have not made it until you have made it in New York.

Alvin Ailey founded a dance company in New York City.

The Statue of Liberty

Boston or New York?

Boston and New York are two early cities that have grown and changed over time. People say they are very different and very much the same. What do you think? Can you tell which city is which?

Learn More About:

Boston and New York

Books

1. Farber, Norma. **As I Was Crossing Boston Common.** 1991. E.P. Dutton.

2. Lasky, Kathryn. **She's Wearing a Dead Bird on Her Head.** 1995. Hyperion Books.

3. Stevens, C. **Lily and Miss Liberty.** 1992. Scholastic.

CD-ROM

Morgan's Adventures in Colonial America. 1996. HarperKids Interactive.

Chicago and Detroit

Chicago and Detroit are in the center of the country. Their locations helped these cities grow as people moved west. In the 1800s, they were important shipping centers. By the early 1900s, both Chicago and Detroit were key factory cities.

Chicago...all roads lead there

The Chicago fire that destroyed the city

Many people attended the World's Fair.

Fire, Fire Everywhere

Just as Chicago was becoming an important city, a huge fire swept through the city. The fire lasted two full days (October 8-9, 1871). It left almost 100,000 people homeless. The city had to be rebuilt. This time builders used stone instead of wood. After the fire, Chicago created the first modern fire department.

At the World's Fair

The World's Fair was held in Chicago in 1893. The 150 buildings were white and looked like Greek temples. It was known as the "White City." The buildings became models for most public buildings built over the next 40 years.

Did you know?

The Oprah Winfrey Show, produced in Chicago, today attracts as many people as once visited the 1893 Chicago World's Fair.

Hog factory workers

Tall, Taller, Tallest Building

The Sears Tower, built between 1970 and 1974, is the tallest office building in the world. It has 110 stories and is 1,454 feet or 790 meters high. It is taller than both the World Trade Center and Empire State Building.

The Sears Tower

Hog Heaven

Chicago became known as "Hog City" because it had so many meat-processing factories. Many immigrants came to Chicago and found work in these factories. Chicago's shipyards and railroads made shipping meat to the East and West Coasts fast and easy.

Did you know?

The first female African-American senator, Carol Moseley Braun, is from Chicago.

Carol Moseley Braun, United States Senator

Detroit... city of cars and music

African-American children
in a science lab

Workers in shipyard

Detroit factory

Education for All

Some African-Americans escaping slavery passed through Detroit on their way to freedom in Canada. After the Civil War many African-Americans moved to Detroit. Detroit became one of the first cities to pass laws that granted equal education for all children, including the newly arrived African-Americans.

Boom, Boom, Boom Times

Because of its key location, Detroit grew fast during the early 1800s. Immigrants from England, Ireland, Germany, and many other countries arrived there. They found jobs working for the railroads and in the lumber and shipyards. Detroit became a city of factories.

Cars, Cars, and More Cars

In the 1900s, cars became a big industry. Almost all of the first cars were made in Detroit. Henry Ford produced the first assembly-line cars there. Soon everyone wanted a car, and factories in Detroit built them.

An early car assembly line

Diana Ross, a Motown star

The Renaissance Center in Detroit

From Motor City to Motown

Another success story for Detroit is Motown Records. Founded in 1960 by Berry Gordy, it made many hit records. Some Motown stars were Diana Ross and the Supremes, Aretha Franklin, and the Temptations. Many of the top ten records in the 1960s and 1970s were by Motown artists.

Rebuilding Downtown Detroit

By the 1960s, many people had moved out of the inner city. Detroit was one of the first cities to rebuild. It built the Renaissance Center. This center has many hotels, twenty-eight restaurants, and numerous shops. It attracts people back into the city.

Chicago and Detroit Today

Many people still work and live in Chicago and Detroit. These cities have survived by changing and rebuilding. How are these two cities alike and different?

Learn More About:

Chicago and Detroit

Books

1. Adoff, Arnold. **Street Music: City Poems**. 1995. Crown.

2. Griffith, Helen. **Grandaddy's Stars**. 1995. Greenwillow Books.

3. Sorensen, Henri. **New Hope**. 1995. Lothrop, Lee & Shepard.

CD-ROM

America Adventure. 1994. Knowledge Adventure.

Where in the USA is Carmen Sandiego? 1992-1994. Broderbund Software, Inc.

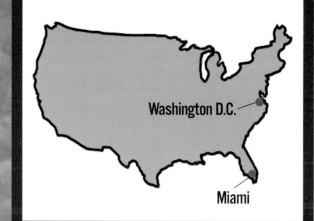

Washington D.C.

Washington D.C. and Miami

Washington D.C. is our nation's capital. It was not always the capital, though. George Washington chose the new site in northern Virginia because it was in the center of the thirteen original colonies.

Miami is the gateway to South America. It is a new city. Many immigrants from Cuba and South America have settled there.

The White House burning

Jacqueline Kennedy in the White House

The East Room

The Most Famous House

The White House was made the home of the President in 1800. Its address is 1600 Pennsylvania Avenue. A contest was held to decide its design. An Irish American, James Hoban, won it. The White House was burned by the British in 1814.

The White House Today

The White House was rebuilt and enlarged after the fire. First Lady Jacqueline Kennedy was the first to make major changes to the interior. She had many antiques restored. Other First Ladies have continued to redecorate the White House.

Did you know?

Abigail Adams hung her laundry in the East Room. Today it is an important room for formal dinners.

The Vietnam Veterans Memorial

Honoring All the People

There are many monuments in Washington D.C. Some monuments, such as the Washington Monument and the Lincoln and Jefferson Memorials, honor presidents. Other monuments, such as the one for the Unknown Soldier and the Vietnam Veterans Memorial, honor soldiers. Many people visit these places.

Did you know?

Maya Lin designed the Vietnam Veterans Memorial. She won a contest to design the monument when she was a twenty-two-year-old college student.

The Nation's Library

The Library of Congress is our nation's library. It holds the records of all books published in the United States. It has over 14 million books and 36 million manuscripts. It also has photos, videos, newspapers, and other materials for a total of 88 million items. The Librarian of Congress is appointed by the President.

This is the Library of Congress.

Miami... a city still growing and changing

Fighting for Freedom

The Spanish built a mission in the Miami area in the 1560s. Later, United States troops built Fort Dallas there. They fought the Seminole Indians for the land. Many Seminoles were sent to Oklahoma, but three hundred escaped. They fought hard for their freedom. Osceola, their leader, kept them free into the 1800s. He died in prison.

This is Osceola, Seminole leader.

Woman Founds Miami

In 1891, Julia Tuttle, a rich widow from the Midwest, settled in the area that would become Miami. She helped get railroads built that linked Miami to the rest of Florida. Miami was ready to become a city.

Did you know?

Alligator wrestling by Seminoles is a tourist attraction. A white farm-boy, Henry Coppinger, Jr., taught them how to do it.

This is Miami Beach in the 1920s.

The Building Boom

Soon oranges were being shipped north, and tourists were coming to Miami. So Tuttle built the Miami Hotel. People saw Miami as a place to make money buying and selling land. Miami created many real estate millionaires. In the 1920s, President Warren Harding spent his winter vacation there. Miami was becoming the "vacation city."

Oranges are the main crop of Florida.

This is a cafe in Little Havana.

Oranges, Orange Bowl, Orange Juice

Oranges became the number-one crop in Florida. Many orange groves were planted around the city. Factories to make juice were built. To celebrate, Miami started the Orange Bowl parade in 1934. Today the Orange Bowl is a big college football game, and the parade is on national television.

Little Havana

Cuba is very close to Miami. In the 1960s, many people left Cuba and moved to Miami. The main street of the Cuban community in Miami is Calle Ocho (Eighth Street). Here there are many stores, coffee houses, and restaurants where Cuban immigrants gather to shop, talk, and spend time.

Did you know?

South Miami beach is called "South Hollywood." The buildings are bright and colorful. Many famous movie stars, models, and recording artists live there.

Washington D.C. and Miami Today

Washington D.C. and Miami are cities that continue to change. Washington changes with every election. Miami changes as new immigrants from Latin America continue to move there. How do you think these cities are alike and different?

Learn More About:

Washington D.C. and Miami

Books

1. DiSalvo-Ryan, D. **City Green**. 1994. William Morrow.

2. Waters, Kate. **The Story of the White House**. 1992. Scholastic

Online Site

Welcome to the White House
http://www.whitehouse.gov/
Visit the White House and its occupants

Santa Fe

Dallas

Dallas and Santa Fe

Dallas is a new city. Dallas is known as the "Big D." Everything there is big. Dallas is known for oil and sports.

Santa Fe is one of the oldest cities in the United States. Many artists live and work in the city.

Early Dallas

The Dallas Cowboys

Oil helped make Dallas a rich city.

From a Trading Post to Malls

In 1841, John Neely Bryan, a lawyer from Tennessee, dug a shelter in what is now Dallas. Neely sold or gave out free lots to settlers. The area became a stagecoach stop. Dallas grew quickly. Today Dallas is the second-largest city in Texas.

Sports, Sports and More Sports

Dallas has four major sports teams. The Dallas Cowboys compete in football and have won several Super Bowl games. The Texas Rangers compete in baseball. And the Mavericks are a National Basketball League team. The city even has a hockey team, the Dallas Stars.

There's Oil in Those Fields

Cotton and the railroads made Dallas an important city. But the discovery of oil near Dallas in 1930 changed it forever. Suddenly people flocked to the area to discover their own "black gold." Few people found oil, but those who did became very rich. And Dallas became known as the "rich city."

Early Fort Worth

The giant state fair in Dallas

The Twin City... Fort Worth

Fort Worth is 30 miles (48.3 kilometers) from Dallas. People often refer to the two cities as one. They share an airport and way of life. Fort Worth began as a fort. It became a cattle town in the 1800s. Then oil replaced cattle as the main industry. Today Fort Worth is a modern city, much like its twin, Dallas.

Did you know?

The Dallas/Fort Worth airport is one of the largest in the United States. Millions of people fly in and out of this airport every year.

A Giant State Fair

Most states have fairs. Dallas has the biggest state fair in the United States. It is held every year in October in Fair Park. More than three million people go to this fair. It has many rides, activities, and stands. You can buy or ride almost anything there.

Santa Fe...the city of adobe houses

Santa Fe... An Old City

Santa Fe was founded in 1609. It is one of the oldest cities in the United States. It was the capital of the Spanish colony of New Mexico. Ancient adobe houses built long ago by the Pueblo Indians are just outside the city. Today many people still build adobe houses.

The Santa Fe Trail

The End of the Santa Fe Trail

The Santa Fe Trail opened in 1821. It began in Independence, Missouri, and ended in Santa Fe, New Mexico. The trail was 780 miles (1255 kilometers) long. By the 1860s, more than 5,000 wagons traveled the trail. People traded manufactured goods for gold, silver, furs, and horses.

A modern adobe house in Santa Fe

Maria and Julian Martinez.

Native Americans selling their work

Did you know?

Santa Fe is known as the "City Different" because of the weaving of three cultures: Native American, Spanish, and Anglo.

The Pueblo Potter

The Pueblo Indians sell their art in Santa Fe. Maria Martinez was a famous Pueblo potter. She was known for her black-on-black designs. Martinez's pottery is in many museums. She was called the "mother of pottery." Today her family carries on her work.

Santa Fe Today

In August, Santa Fe holds the Indian Fair where Pueblo and Navajo craftspeople sell their work. Many people visit Santa Fe to buy jewelry, pottery, rugs, and other handicrafts from the Indian craftspeople. They wear their traditional clothes as they sell their goods.

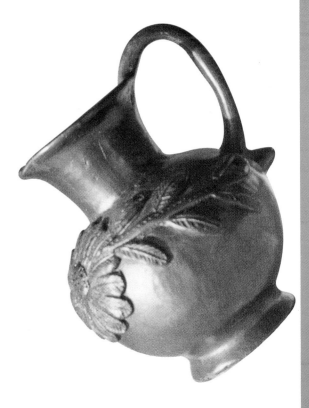

Pueblo pottery

25

Dallas and Santa Fe are both important cities in the southwestern part of the United States. Dallas is a new city, known for its wealth. Santa Fe is an old city, known for its artists and adobe houses. How do you think these cities are alike and different?

Dallas and Santa Fe Today

Learn More About:

Dallas and Santa Fe

Books

1. Fanelli, Sara. **My Map Book**. 1995. HarperCollins.

2. Johnson, Stephen. **Alphabet City**. 1995. Viking Press.

CD-ROM

Sim City Classic. 1989 . Maxis Software.

Online Site

U.S. Census Bureau. http://census.gov Find out how many people live in cities across the U.S.

Seattle

San Francisco

San Francisco and Seattle

San Francisco and Seattle are both cities by the ocean. Their location helped them become important tourist cities. San Francisco is known for its chocolate, Chinatown, and cable cars. Seattle is known for its coffee, Space Needle, and seafood. San Francisco is a city full of history and hills. Seattle is a city by the mountains with a growing computer industry.

San Francisco... the city by the bay

Early San Francisco

Gold miners

Tent City

Explorers Sir Francis Drake and Juan Carillo sailed right past San Francisco Bay. But in 1775, Gaspar de Portolo claimed the San Francisco area for Spain. In 1835, the United States tried to buy the area, but Spain would not sell. An Englishman set up a tent made from his sails there. That was the city. In 1846, the United States took over the area. There was no resistance. The tent city was named San Francisco.

There's Gold in Them There Hills

San Francisco remained a frontier city until 1848. Then gold was discovered. Suddenly 80,000 prospectors went there. People dreamed of becoming rich. Very few found much gold. San Francisco became a wild place, full of gamblers, pirates, and outlaws.

Chinese children in San Francisco in the late 1800s

The Chinese Settle in San Francisco

Many Chinese people arrived in 1849. They hoped to strike it rich by finding gold. Then they would be able to return to China very rich. Few found gold. The Chinese panned for gold in teams. Laws were passed to prevent this. Many Chinese stayed in San Francisco. Today it has the largest Chinese American community in the United States.

The Quake of 1906

On April 18, 1906, at 5:12 a.m., a great earthquake hit San Francisco. It killed more than 400 people. The earthquake caused a fire that destroyed 28,000 buildings. The city had to be rebuilt. New buildings now have steel frames. This helps to keep them standing during earthquakes.

Did you know?

Fisherman's Wharf was a commerical fishing port. It was built by Italian immigrants in the 1800s. Today it is a row of restaurants, shops, and motels.

The fire and earthquake of 1906

Seattle... the city of mountains and water

Trees, Trees, and Lumber

Seattle was named for an Indian chief who helped the early settlers from Illinois. Henry Yesler, a lumberman, built a sawmill there around 1853. Soon Seattle was producing lumber and paper. These mills offered jobs to the incoming settlers. Seattle became a growing city.

Early Seattle

Early logging in Seattle

Gold, Lumber, and a Good Port

Seattle is located on Puget Sound, a waterway that links the city to the Pacific Ocean. This location made Seattle a good port city. With the Klondike and Alaska gold rush of 1897 and 1898, Seattle became an important shipping city. Many goods were shipped to the miners from Seattle. Today Seattle ships goods to the Far East and Alaska.

Bill Gates

From the Space Needle to Mountains

Tourists enjoy visiting Seattle. In 1962, Seattle had a World's Fair. One of the main buildings of the Fair was a giant Space Needle. This building with a restaurant on the top attracts many people. Some also visit Mount Rainier, which can be seen from the Space Needle.

From Lumber to Aircraft to Microsoft

Seattle developed new industries as it grew. In 1916, William Boeing started the Boeing Company, which became a leading aircraft manufacturer. Recently Bill Gates founded Microsoft there. Microsoft is a giant computer software firm. Today many people have jobs in the lumber, shipping, aircraft, and software industries.

Modern Seattle

Did you know?

Mount Rainier is Washington's highest mountain. It is 14,410 feet(4,392 meters) high. Each year many hikers climb to the top. It is one of Seattle's famous landmarks.

31

San Francisco and Seattle Today

Both San Francisco and Seattle are important port cities. Their locations have helped them to grow and prosper. And both are popular tourist cities. How do you think these cities are alike and different?

Learn More About:

San Francisco and Seattle

Books

1. Climo, S. **City! San Francisco**. 1990. Macmillan.

2. Cosgrove, S. **Wheedle On the Needle**. 1975. Allan Publishers, Inc.

Online Sites

Seismic Information
http://www.geophys.washington.edu/seismosurfing.html
Learn about earthquakes and seismic activity.